THE ADVENTURES
of
BABY BEAR

Text by Aubrey Lang
Photography by Wayne Lynch

**FIFTH
HOUSE**

THE ADVENTURES
of BABY BEAR

The publisher gratefully acknowledges the support of The Canada Council for the Arts
and the Department of Canadian Heritage.

We acknowledge the financial support of the Government of Canada
through the Book Publishing Industry Development Program for our publishing activities.

Design: Wycliffe Smith Design Inc.
Printed in Hong Kong
01 02 03 04 05/5 4 3 2 1

CANADIAN CATALOGUING IN PUBLICATION DATA
Lang, Aubrey
The adventures of Baby Bear

ISBN 1-894004-71-X

1.Black bear—Juvenile literature. I. Lynch, Wayne. II. Title.
QL737.C27L36 2001   j599.78'5139   C2001-910168-6

Fifth House Ltd.
A Fitzhenry & Whiteside Company
1511-1800 4th Street SW
Calgary, AB T2S 2S5
1-800-387-9776

D I D   Y O U   K N O W ?

- Bears prepare for winter by eating and eating. They may put on over two pounds (one kilogram) of fat every day. If you wanted to eat as much, you would have to gobble down forty-three hamburgers and twelve large orders of French fries every day!

- Black bears eat mostly grass, wildflowers, nuts, berries and insects.

- The largest black bear ever caught was a male from Manitoba that weighed 805 pounds (365 kilograms). That's heavier than most families!

- Bears hibernate—they don't eat, drink, urinate, defecate or move around much, but they will spend the winter napping. Most black bears hibernate for four to six months but some bears in Alaska stay in their winter dens for over eight months every year!

- Bear dens are not large caves. Most are just big enough for the bear to squeeze inside. A small den is easier for the bear to warm up with its body heat.

- Bears mate in early summer, but the babies don't develop inside the mother's body until autumn. The pregnancy will continue only if the mother is fat and healthy enough.

- The cubs are born in the winter den. Only bears give birth while they hibernate.

- Black bears normally have two or three cubs in a litter, but some older mothers might have as many as six cubs.

- Black bear cubs stay with their mother until they are eighteen months old.

After play the cubs fill up on milk then fall asleep on their mother's soft fur.

The bear cubs play and nap many times during the day. Each day they get bigger, braver and stronger.

Soon the cubs will be able to follow their mother through the forest.

The second brother climbs a tree stump. He reaches the top but can't get down again.

The cub calls out for his mother, his cry is just like a human baby's.

Mother bear arrives, lifts the frightened cub in her jaws and gently carries him back to the nest.

When the brothers wake up, they also set out to explore.

One brother climbs an old log near the nest. He sniffs and scratches the soft wood with his claws.

But the little cub is new to climbing. He slips and rolls off the log, then runs back to the safety of his mother.

The next morning the female cub is the first one to wake up.

The dried leaves feel crunchy under her paws. She runs through the leaves and rolls in them.

Play helps the cubs build strong muscles and bones.

Still drowsy from her winter hibernation, the mother bear falls asleep.

In their new nest, the cubs are too excited to sleep. They stay awake, looking around until it is dark.

Outside the winter den there are many dangers, but the little cubs are safe as long as they stay close to their mother.

When the air begins to chill, the mother bear returns and leads the cubs to a new home.

The place is close to their winter den. It's a nest of branches, leaves and dried grasses that their mother has raked into a pile on the ground.

In their new home it will be easier for the cubs to run around and play.

The smallest of the three cubs is alone inside the den.

When he is ready, he climbs outside to join his brother and sister.

The forest is much bigger than a den. It's a strange world filled with new sounds and smells. So at first the three cubs stay close together.

The sun feels warm on the cub's fur.

She can smell the forest for the first time, and she is curious. She crawls onto a rock, followed by one brother.

A big black crow flies overhead and caws. Frightened, the little cubs duck their heads.

But soon they are ready to explore again.

Today the cubs have been left alone for the first time.

The mother bear hasn't eaten for many months. She has gone outside to search for food.

The den seems big and empty now, and the cubs huddle together to keep each other warm.

The female cub is bolder than her brothers. She sticks her nose outside the den.

Not all black bears have black fur like this family.

Some have brown fur and some have white, even when their mother is completely black.

All bear cubs have blue eyes, but their eyes turn brown by the time they are a year old.

When the cubs have finished nursing, the mother licks their bottoms with her long, wet tongue. This makes the cubs urinate and defecate.

Then the mother drinks the urine and eats the stools. In this way she keeps the winter den clean.

The baby bears nurse five or six times a day.

The mother's milk is as thick as whipped cream. The cubs will grow quickly on these rich, fatty meals.

Each cub has its own nipple to drink from, and when they feed, they make a loud humming sound. If you could stand outside their winter den, you would hear them.

The cubs are now two months old, and they are the size of small dogs.

Their mother is still sleepy, but the cubs are full of energy as they play and wrestle with each other.

The cubs climb all over their mother's back, using their sharp claws to crawl through her thick fur. They are ready to leave the family's winter den.

It's Christmas in the forest, and it is snowing. Hidden in a shelter of boulders under the deep snow is a family of black bears.

The mother has given birth to three tiny cubs. Each cub is no bigger than a squirrel.

Mother bear curls her large body around the cubs to keep them safe and warm. The family spends all winter like this.

Then one day in early spring it's time to leave.